Flowing in Favor

*Inspiring Girls in Spiritual Growth,
Grace, and Greatness*

KAREN POWELL

ISBN 979-8-89428-048-6 (paperback)
ISBN 979-8-89428-058-5 (digital)

Copyright © 2024 by Karen Powell

All rights reserved. No part of this publication may be reproduced, distributed, or transmitted in any form or by any means, including photocopying, recording, or other electronic or mechanical methods without the prior written permission of the publisher. For permission requests, solicit the publisher via the address below.

Christian Faith Publishing
832 Park Avenue
Meadville, PA 16335
www.christianfaithpublishing.com

Printed in the United States of America

Contents

Foreword v

Acknowledgments vii

Introduction ix

Flowing in Spiritual Growth 1

Pause and Pray 6

#honorParents 14

Dream, Believe, and Achieve 19

Blessed in the Skin I'm In 24

Designed for Generational Blessings 27

Love Your Peace 30

Growing in Grace 32

Healing for a Heavy Heart 35

Forgiveness for Me 38

Respect Yourself and Others 42

Friendships 45

Acts of Kindness 48

Academic Success 50

Destined for Greatness 52

Scriptures to Ponder 55

Conclusion 59

References 61

Foreword

This book is a great resource for young ladies, parents, and their mentors, coaches, and parents, whether you are raising biological, adopted, or foster children. Much of the frustration parents experience during parenting comes from a lack of knowledge or a lack of practical action steps for engaging in the faith during child-rearing. Dr. Karen Powell has done an exceptional job of creating this book as a resource for parenting and for training up young ladies. This book exposes Dr. Karen's heart for seeing young ladies grow up to live a life that is pleasing to God.

Her unique and innocent style of writing will captivate you and renew your mind regarding God's will for the life of young ladies as they meditate on each chapter. In this book, you will learn how to pray to flow in favor, become inspired, grow spiritually in grace, and greatness. You will also learn scriptures regarding God's promise for young ladies. Most importantly, you will discover the principle of faith confession so you can speak what God says.

This book is also a tool to teach young ladies who they are in Christ Jesus.

Finally, this book is Dr. Karen's way of answering the call to advance. I encourage you as the reader to answer that same call by learning and applying the principles con-

Karen Powell

tained inside each chapter that you may "flow in favor and inspire girls in spiritual growth, grace, and greatness."

Elder Cornelia Coleman

Acknowledgments

First, giving obedience to the Lord our God for the great and mighty things He does. God is so wonderful, and He deserves all praise, glory, and honor! For it would not have been possible for me to complete His work and inspire our young spirits, except His grace and favor were upon me, so I am truly grateful! I want to thank my family for being generous and allowing me the time spent away from them to complete this work. A big thank-you to my loving husband, Cloyd, who is my inspiration with his unwavering love and compassionate spirit; you keep me full of laughter with a young spirit.

I'm so thankful for my tenacious daughter, Teren, my mini-me, for your support and thoughtfulness as you listened compassionately throughout this process. Additionally, I'm grateful to our other adult children through marriage—Demond, Tiffany, Yvette, Jessica, Joy, and Xavier—for your support. To my one and only brother, Melvin, my bestie who always encourages me in a jovial manner; thank you for your ear! A special shout-out to all of my family and friends who have encouraged me on this journey. I'm truly blessed to be in the Reed and Herring legacy.

The Lord knows that I'm ever so thankful for my prayer family, the 5:00 a.m., 8:00 p.m., and Apouringin2 prayer warriors; and I thank the Lord for you each day. We know the effective, fervent prayers of the righteous avails much! Thanking the Lord for my spiritual big sister, Elder Cornelia, who has been instrumental in the women's ministry. Once again, thank you to everyone that has given me an encouraging word.

Introduction

First and foremost, with a grateful heart, I am inspired that you have picked up this book. It is not by chance that you've come upon it. Whether you are reading this book as a purchase for yourself, or as a gift to someone else, you were supposed to possess and read this book. By divine intervention, you are the right person selecting the right book at the right time to read and be blessed by the Lord. May your reading enhance your godly wisdom, knowledge, and understanding with blessings to inspire you in spiritual growth, grace, and greatness in the Lord. It is the Lord's will for you to do great and wonderful things as you take heed to His word and that which is reflected herein.

As I write this book, it has given me great pleasure to speak to your heart so I can encourage you as my daughter, the girl within, my little sister in the Lord, and my special mentee. You are blessed by the Lord, and I truly thank and encourage you to be the best you! If you didn't know, you do know now! You are wonderful, and God's Word declares that you are fearfully and wonderfully made in God's image. Marvelous are His works, and our soul knows this right well (Psalm 139:14). This book is written to inspire you to be all that God created you to be and to do that which will bless Him, and in turn, you will be blessed also!

Flowing in Spiritual Growth

Hello, greatness! My dear spiritual daughter, look what the Lord is doing for you and through you. The secret is out; and you must know that your spiritual growth is the most important thing you will need in this life! It is more important than each breath that you take. For it is our Father God who gives you breath in your body. Keeping it real, your spiritual growth is more important than food or clothing, money, silver, gold, or diamonds. Yes, food and clothing are necessary earthly things that you must have, but it's not more important than your spiritual growth in the Lord. When it comes to your spiritual growth, you are like a newborn baby. It's important for you to crave or desire the pure spiritual milk of the Word of God so that by it you may grow up in your salvation (1 Peter 2:2). Oh, taste and see that the Lord is good; blessed is the one who takes refuge in him (Psalm 34:8).

Don't believe the false hype that you don't have to accept Jesus Christ as your Lord and Savior. Satan is a master liar, and many young people have fallen victim to the deceit. In order to grow spiritually and have fellowship with God, you must believe in His Son Jesus Christ and have a personal relationship with Him. Stay strong in your conviction of serving Jesus, as it will allow you to grow spiritually, and make every attempt to study God's Word to apply it to your life each and every day.

Our Heavenly Father wants us all to grow up in His grace and knowledge. The Lord instructs parents to "train up a child in the way he or she should go; and when they are old, they will not depart from it" (Proverbs 22:6). As I was growing up as a young girl, my mother often reminded me to remember being trained up in the way of the Lord. Fast-forwarding years later, as a parent myself, I'm reminded of the one important aspect of parenting that includes raising children up knowing who God is so that our children may also have a personal relationship with Him. As you continue reading this book, may the Lord God stir up His Spirit in you.

I'm encouraged by faith to know that you are being nurtured in your spiritual growth. Your spiritual growth will be increased, because it pleases the Father our God when we grow closer to him. 2 Peter 3:18 tells us to "grow in the grace and knowledge of our Lord and Savior Jesus Christ." As you grow spiritually and draw closer to the Father, it will be His favor upon you to give you increase in your faith and in every area of your life.

Flowing in Favor

Young sister, this doesn't mean that you will be perfect or that you won't experience making bad decisions or unwise choices. Of course, we are human and sometimes we mess up and make mistakes, but please remember this one thing. The Lord will perfect that which concerns you (Psalm 138:8a). You must remember that you are not alone; the Spirit of God lives within you. There may be times when you will be tempted to sin, and you may even question your faith. Continue to trust in the Lord our God during these times, and be careful what you listen to and participate in. Turn away from, reject, and denounce any evil, wicked, or demonic activity or entity that disobeys, rejects, or exalts itself above the Word of God.

My prayer for you is that you study the Word of God. Studying and meditating on scriptures will increase your knowledge of the Lord our God and Savior Jesus Christ. It will strengthen your trust in Him. There are so many methods for you to read and study the Bible, such as using a paperbound Holy Bible, using a phone app, or listening to audio versions of the Bible. The point is that you have a choice to feed your soul with things that are holy and righteous and be encouraged to choose growth in the Lord.

Be encouraged and appreciate that the favor of God is upon you and His righteousness and truth dwells within you. I'm just a vessel being used by our awesome God to stir up the gift inside of you and encourage you to walk in the favor of God that is flowing within you. You can live and increase in spiritual growth, because it pleases the Father. Go on and take the leap of faith and grow in grace as a child of the Most High God, being fully aware that you shall excel in greatness!

The *ABCs* Concerning Your Spiritual Growth

A – Alpha   The Lord Jehovah is Alpha, the first and beginning of all things (Revelation 1:8).

B – Beginning   In the beginning was the Word, and the Word was with and is God (John 1:1).

C – Creator   God is the Creator, and through Him all things are made (John 1:3).

D – Disciple   People know I'm a disciple of Christ, because I love others (John 13:35).

E – El Shaddai Almighty God El Shaddai, I will walk before you blameless (Genesis 17:1).

F – Faith   I will walk by faith and not by sight (2 Corinthians 5:7).

G – Goodness   Goodness and mercy shall follow me all the days of my life (Psalm 23:6).

H – Help   My help comes from the Lord, the Maker of heaven and earth (Psalm 121:1).

I – Idol   I will not worship or serve any idols, because the Lord is my God (Exodus 20:5).

J – Jesus   I confess with my mouth, "Jesus is Lord," and He is my Savior (Romans 10:9).

K – King   Jesus Christ is the King of glory; His kingdom will have no end (Isaiah 9:7).

L – Lord   The Lord is my rock, my fortress, and the One who rescues me (Psalm 18:2).

M – Mercy   God shows mercy to the merciful (Matthew 5:7).

N – Needs   But my God shall supply all your need according to his riches in glory by Christ Jesus (Philippians 4:19).

Flowing in Favor

O – Overcome The Light overcomes the darkness; Jesus is that Light (John 1:5).

P – Persevere Blessed is the one who perseveres under trial because, having stood the test, that person will receive the crown of life that the Lord has promised to those who love him (James 1:12).

Q – Quicken Plead my cause and deliver me: quicken me according to thy word (Psalm 119:154).

R – Righteous The Lord is righteous in all his ways and faithful in all he does (Psalm 145:17).

S – Saved For by grace you have been saved through faith. And this is not your own doing; it is the gift of God (Ephesians 2:8).

T – Thanks Oh give thanks to the Lord, for he is good, for his steadfast love endures forever (Psalm 107:1).

U – Understand And the peace of God, which surpasses all understanding, will guard your hearts and your minds in Christ Jesus (Philippians 4:7).

V – Victory But thanks be to God, which giveth us the victory through our Lord Jesus Christ (1 Corinthians 15:57).

W – Winner With God on our side we will win; He will defeat our enemies (Psalm 108:13).

X – X-ray God is providing me with X-ray-type vision and wisdom to respond and not blinded by sin.

Y – Yield Neither yield ye your members as instruments of unrighteousness unto sin: but yield yourselves unto God.

Z – Zealous Because I have been freed from sin and its power, I am zealous and passionate to do good works (Titus 2:14).

Pause and Pray

Prayer is one of the most important things that you can commit to! Commit to praying each day. You can pray at any time of day. Prayer is your communication with the Father, our God. It's that quiet personal moment where you give your attention to the Lord in conversation with Him. If you don't know how to pray, just say, "Lord, have mercy on me." God looks at our heart, so do not be overly concerned with the words that you say if you are not familiar or used to praying. The important thing is that you begin praying every day if you don't already.

Prayer can be short and sweet, or it can be long. Prayer can be in the form of a song, or just meditating about God. You can pray anywhere and at any time, but remember the important thing is that you pray every day! You may choose to bow your head, or you may want to look up to the heav-

Flowing in Favor

ens if it's appropriate or safe. You may close your eyes or keep them open. Lifting your hands is a form of surrender to God, which is perfectly fine. Clapping your hands and stomping your feet are also awesome demonstrations of praise when you pray.

You may wonder, why do I need to pray? Or you may wonder why is prayer important? The first reason is because the Bible says that people should always pray and never quit praying (1 Thessalonians 5:17 NKJV). The second reason we should pray every day is because prayer changes things. The Bible says the effective, fervent prayers of the righteous avails much (James 5:16 NKJV). This means prayer can change your situation. When you pray, prayer begins to shift things in your life. When you do pray, believe that the Lord our God hears your prayers. He hears every prayer. Whether you are praying aloud, softly, or just meditating and praying from your heart in secret, our Father, the Lord, will hear your prayers, because they come from your heart.

Some people cry when they pray. Years ago, I was told that God catches every tear. Tears may come from hurt and pain, or they flow from one rejoicing and being grateful for who God is in our life. Whenever you pray, and whatever you pray for, believe that God is making provision for you and will take care of you. In your prayer, remember to give God thanks. Thanking God is a form of praise. Praise God because He is such a great and awesome Father. So keep praying, believing, and loving the Lord our God. You can pause right now and give God glory. Just take a few seconds to tell God thank-you for taking care of you.

Do you know that the Lord already knows everything you have going on in your life? Yes, your life matters to

God! And He can provide for every one of your needs, hallelujah! There are so many reasons why we should pray, young beautiful sisters! You should always pray for yourself to have a closer relationship with the Father. Pray for parents, siblings, friends, neighbors, and anyone important to you that they also believe in the Lord Jesus and have a personal relationship with the Lord.

It's important to pray for schools, and include all the students, teachers, principals and vice principals, cafeteria workers, counselors, coaches, and all who have authority over the students in elementary, middle or junior high, and high schools. Pray for safety in our schools, on the school buses, and for all those who make decisions regarding the educational systems. Pray for healing and deliverance for those who are special in your life. It's also important to pray for those you may not even know who may be dealing with life-threatening situations. Pray for our military soldiers, police officers, firemen, astronauts, and judges. You can pray for our healthcare workers, teachers, social workers, and our social service system.

Each day you need peace, strength, and joy, therefore pray to the Lord, because he is waiting to answer you. "And pray in the Spirit on all occasions with all kinds of prayers and requests. With this in mind, be alert and always keep on praying for all the Lord's people" (Ephesians 6:18 NIV). Yes, God will hear your prayers, my wonderful little sisters, so please take the time to pray every day. Just as oxygen is important for us to breathe and live, so too is prayer for every child of the Lord. It's extremely important for every believer of the Lord to pray. The First Epistle to the Thessalonians 5:16–18 reads, "Rejoice always, pray with-

Flowing in Favor

out ceasing [do not quit praying], give thanks in all circumstances; for this is the will of God in Christ Jesus for you."

Jesus prayed during His ministry on earth. Also, Jesus encouraged His disciples to pray, which many refer to as the model prayer, according to Matthew 6:9–13 ESV, "Pray then like this: Our Father in heaven, hallowed be Your name. Your kingdom come, Your will be done, on earth as it is in heaven. Give us this day our daily bread, and forgive us our debts, as we also have forgiven our debtors. And lead us not into temptation but deliver us from evil." This is not just for parents or older people to pray. The Lord wants young people to stretch their faith in prayer and call on Him. That's correct, God hears and answers the prayers of young people, and it's always encouraging to know that young people are praying for this world and others.

The Bible says that the Lord is our refuge (shelter) and strength, a very present help in time of trouble (Psalm 46:1). Aren't you glad that we have a helper at all times? The Holy Father loves us so much that He sent His Holy Son. Jesus loves us so much that He died for us, and He did not stay dead, young sister. Hallelujah! That's right, the Son of God, Jesus Christ, rose from the grave on the third day with all power in His hands so we could be reconciled back to the Father, our God.

Jesus is the King of glory, and He reigns forevermore! Jesus is sitting at the right hand of the Father God making intercession for us (Romans 8:34). And when you pray your prayer, conclude, "in Jesus's mighty name!" There is power in His name, Holy Ghost power. The Bible tells us that when we call upon the name of Jesus, demons will tremble and flee from us. What better time to practice than now? Right now is an acceptable time for you to call upon the mighty name of Jesus. Jesus dwells with you when you acknowledge Him and call upon His wonderful name. Pause and ask Jesus, our precious Lamb of God who takes away the sins of the world, to forgive you of all sins and give God the glory in Jesus's Name!

Is there anything that you need? Do you need healing in your body? Do you need to have a better relationship with your parents or siblings? Do you feel you should be doing better in school? Whatever is on your heart, prayers work! By all means, do not downplay prayer. Prayers change things. But you must have faith. Faith is the substance of things hoped for and the evidence of things not seen (Hebrews 11:1 KJV). Be ready to receive that which you ask of the Lord. It may not come just as you ask, because sometimes one must wait as the Lord knows the right timing but keep praying and stay in faith and see how the Lord blesses and answers your prayers.

As you begin to pray and talk with the Lord more and more, your prayers may become more personal as you pray to the Lord about things that are on your heart. You may even desire to encourage your family and friends to pray. I've heard the saying, "Much prayer, much power. Little prayer, little power." It's also good when you have a prayer partner or a prayer group. I've been a part of a prayer group for more than thirty years. My prayer partners and I pray every morning at five o'clock. I became a member of this prayer group when I was only twenty-four years old. I was the youngest member for many years, but now there is another prayer partner who is younger than me. We are known as the 5:00 a.m. Prayer Line. We have seen so many

Flowing in Favor

prayers answered and experienced miracles happen just because of our faith and prayers.

If you do choose a prayer partner, pray and ask the Lord to guide you to the right person to be in agreement with you in righteousness according to the will of God. Remember, you can pray about anything. God is a very present help in time of trouble, so if you are troubled about anything, the Lord is waiting with outstretched arms and listening ears to be a comfort and help for you, because the Lord our God really, really loves you! It doesn't matter who you may think doesn't love you, Jesus Christ our Lord and God loves you. He loves your soul, so you are not alone.

Prayers of thanksgiving are your praise! My dear little sisters, thank God for everything! He loves for His children to thank Him and praise Him. The Bible says, "Let everything that hath breath praise the Lord (Psalm 150:6 KJV)." It also says, "In everything give thanks, for this is the will of God in Christ Jesus (1 Thessalonians 5:18)." You can thank the Lord as soon as you wake up in the morning, and honestly, it should be the first thing that you do in the morning.

When you leave the house to go anywhere, it is a good idea for you to pray for God's traveling grace and mercy. You can also pray when you get to your destination and thank God for blessing you to get there safely. You can give thanks to God for your family, for your health and strength, for your home, and everything else. Again, there are so many reasons and things to pray for. Truly, I cannot think or name them all. As for praise, the Bible says if we had ten thousand tongues, that still wouldn't be enough for all the blessings of the Lord. I'm encouraging you sisters, pray, pray, and continue to pray. Pray always. *Your prayers will change things!* I'm shouting for you right now, because you are going to experience the power of the Lord Jesus through your prayers. *Hallelujah!*

If you are having problems at school, you can pray to the Lord to be your avenger. He will fight your battles for you. The Bible says that our enemies shall not prevail over us. God has our back. Do you believe that? That's right, the Lord loves us so much that He has our back, and that is enough for us to give Him thanks and praise. Neither the devil nor his demons can prevent us from receiving the love of our Lord and Savior Jesus Christ. Thank God for the blood; there is power in the blood of Jesus Christ, so pray and praise Him for His powerful blood. Keep your eyes on Him. He is with you; and He won't leave you, and don't you leave Him. Pray always. The more you pray, the more you will want to pray.

Lived Experience of a Fourteen-Year-Old Girl

I remember hearing my mother pray, and she would tell me about God. I believed in heaven and hell because at church I heard of it, and I knew that I did not want to go to hell. I was sitting at home one evening and began asking God if He was real, would He come into my life? I invited God into my heart and life and asked Him to hear my prayer because I didn't want to go to hell. I believe that God heard me and that I am saved in Jesus's name. I had a choice, and I chose God!

Flowing in Favor

Points you should know about your prayer flow

1. God hears you when you pray!
2. It is God's will for you to pray!
3. Begin to pray about everything!
4. Prayer changes things!

#honorParents

Children, honor your parents! This is one of the first commandments that God speaks to you and your character as it relates to your actions toward your parents. This commandment isn't just for little children. A person may be twenty years old or older, but you are still your parent's child. Never feel that you are so grown that you do not have to honor your parents. If you want the blessings of the Lord to be upon you, please give respect and honor to your mother, father, and those trusted adults who are helping to raise you.

Despite what you think, parental guidance is crucial for your growth and development. Every good parent has an obligation to raise their child. Your parents have experiences that may benefit you and ensure your journey doesn't include some of the valleys that they may have traveled. Be grateful for parents who love you enough to correct you

Flowing in Favor

when you need it. Parents have a responsibility to lead and guide their children to make decisions that are morally correct, honest, just, and respectful. I'll go a step further and say that you should honor your grandparents. Trust me, this is right in the sight of the Lord. Your obedience and respect to them will take you a very long way. It will bless your life.

You are encouraged to honor your parents because God commands that you honor them. In fact, it is important that you respect all adults. This means you must be respectful in how you answer and talk to your parents. It also means that you should not roll your eyes or talk back to your parents. Some young people believe if they don't mouth off in their parents' presence and talk about them behind their backs, that they're not being disrespectful, but I beg to differ. It's still disrespectful. If you feel that you want to do these things, ask God for the Holy Spirit's help. He says that He is a very present help in times of trouble (Psalm 46:1 ESV).

The blessings of the Lord are upon you, and God gives you the strength to honor and be obedient to your parents. When children are disobedient, they make a conscious decision to dishonor and/or be disrespectful. Your parents may not be able to give you all the things that you desire or want, but God will see that you have everything that you need. And if you don't think that's reason enough to honor your parents, then please honor God. When you honor your parents, you're obeying and honoring God's Word, and you will receive His blessings for your obedience, because in obedience you gain more than you think you are losing.

If you've been disobedient or disrespectful to your parents, pray and ask the Lord to forgive you and create in you a pure heart with love for your parents. You can even ask God for deliverance from any negative influences that may have influenced your disobedience. Ask the Father to open your eyes and heart each day to honor your parents. And as you abide in the Father and He abides in you, the Holy Spirit will inspire you to humble yourself and show honor to your father whether he is in your life or not, and this will be a blessing and impact your life more than you can imagine. Go ahead and ask your dear mother for forgiveness and tell her that you've had a talk with the Lord Jesus and will make every effort to honor and obey her.

It's very disappointing to parents when their children are rebellious. In other words, when a young person settles in their mind, heart, and actions that they are not going to obey the requests, rules, or authority of their parents, they are being rebellious. When a child rebels against their parent(s), they are also rebelling against God. So ask the Lord for forgiveness and ask this of your parents also. Let your parents know that you will strive to be obedient, honorable, and respectful to them.

If you are not being raised by your biological parents, those who are your guardians may be considered your parents. This may be a grandparent, aunt, uncle, or even an older sibling. Even if you may be raised by a foster parent, or a friend's parents, the same principle applies. It's critical for you to understand that you must honor and obey the person or persons who are in the role of being your parent as they provide for your safety, physical, emotional, and spiritual wellbeing. Be thankful for trusting and loving parents because it is a blessing. Always honor them for loving you and always looking out for what's best for you.

Examples of dishonoring your parents include not listening to them when they are speaking with you, or acting like you're ignoring them. If you are in their presence, you should show interest in what they're saying by paying attention to them. When you raise your voice, argue, or talk back to your parent, you are being disrespectful. Even if you don't agree with your parents, you should not disrespect them in this manner. You should refrain from rolling your eyes at your parents, even if they don't recognize this is what you're doing.

Stomping and slamming doors is no way to get your point across. Never, ever curse or use profanity when talking with your parents, and do not ever raise your hand to hit or fight your parents. This is the utmost dishonor and disrespect to your parents. Don't find it surprising if parents punish you when you throw tantrums by complaining, yelling, stomping, or intentionally ignoring them. The Bible instructs parents in Proverbs 29:17, "Discipline your child and he or she will give you rest; he or she will give delight to your heart." Also, Proverbs 13:24 reads, "He who spares the rod hates his son, but he who loves him is careful to discipline him."

Lying to your parents is also dishonorable, so just tell the truth. When you've destroyed the foundation of trust with your parents because you've lied continuously, the consequences may be that your parents will second guess things you say when you may really need to confide in them in truth. So do not get in the habit of lying, and always be honest with your parents. You can show honor to your parents by responding in a positive manner and giving heed to their request. Remember to give your parents hugs and kisses and tell them how much you appreciate and love them. This truly means the world to your parents!

Karen Powell

Under Your Wings
(by Ruth Marie)

You took my heart for safekeeping,
I didn't even have to ask,
Before you even knew me, my mind, or my heart,
You were up for the task.
You kissed me, loved me, held me,
Hugged me—as most good mothers do.
I've never had to question, ever,
If your love is true.
As graceful as the cat that walks,
Or the canary that sings, if only you knew
The true elegance your presence brings.
Forever and always, I'll remain under your wings.

Dream, Believe, and Achieve

Destined for Greatness!

What are your dreams? Is there a burning desire in your heart of what you want to do with your life and what you want out of your life? It is my prayer that you believe in your dreams and know that they can become your reality. That's right, be a dream chaser! If you dream and believe in your dreams, then have the faith and determination to make it your personal goal to achieve them. When I was a youth, I often heard the phrase, "You must believe to achieve."

Young ladies, I believe your dreams are attainable, but do you? It is your choice to believe that your dreams are attainable. You were born with purpose, and it is so important for you to keep dreaming and believing that God will bless you to succeed. Know that He who started a wonderful great work in you is faithful to perform every one of your dreams. Can you believe that? Our God has an outstanding track record. He's done it for so many, and I know that He can and will make it happen for you if you keep dreaming and believing in Him. Do you believe?

God is not the author of confusion, so if you believe, you must walk in faith and work to make the dreams become your reality. Keep in mind, God will give you everything that you need to accomplish your dreams, goals, and aspirations. I'm a living witness and have a testimony that the God we serve can bless your dreams, goals, and aspirations, according to Ephesians 3:20, "Now unto Him that is able to do exceeding abundantly, above all that we ask or think, according to the power that works within us."

Humble beginnings are fine. I repeat, humble beginnings are just fine! It doesn't matter where you come from, or the circumstances in which you currently live. Do not be ashamed of your humble beginnings. Your story may not be everyone's story, but it will bring God glory if you trust in Him to prepare and be with you as you strive to accomplish your dreams, goals, and aspirations. It really doesn't matter if you grow up in a housing development or a mansion. Whether you're from a single-parent home, living with both parents, or perhaps not raised by your biological parents, God still has a plan for your life. Trust Him and acknowledge that He knows your ending as much as your beginning, and trust your dreams are not too big for the God that we serve. As a matter of fact, God specializes in accomplishing those dreams that seem too unbelievable, if only you believe!

What is it that you've been wanting to do? Let the Lord our God stir up the gift within you. If you dream it, or see yourself in it, then you can be it and do it! I encourage you to not let your dreams die. In addition to keeping those dreams written on the pages of your heart, my dear younger sisters, I want to encourage you to write them down on paper or in your journals. I for one am not going to tell you that it will be easy for you to accomplish your dreams, but God promised that your dreams will become a reality if you never give up on Him and His ability to help you accomplish those dreams if you continue to pursue them each and every day.

Your dreams are going to take personal commitment. Just a little commitment each day, and a talk with the Lord about them will give you just what is needed. I remember when I was a little girl and my mother would always tell me about the story *The Little Train That Could*. In this story, it wasn't easy getting up that mountain, but that little train was committed to giving it all he had, and he didn't stop even when it became hard or nearly impossible. That little train kept thinking "I can, I can, I can," and it did. I'll go a step further and ask that you say to yourself, "I can, I can, I can," while thinking of the scripture found in Philippians 4:13, "I can do all things through Christ who strengthens me."

One thing that I do when I set my mind and heart on accomplishing a dream, goal, or desire is to create a vision board. I also write down my dreams and desires in a journal and look at them and meditate on how God will bless me to accomplish them. Dare to dream, and put that dream on paper, like in a journal or a vision board. You can then do extra and pray over it. Now, begin seeing yourself walk in your dreams. That's right, let your faith and God's blessings begin to give life to your dream. The Lord will give you insight, and then you must do the work. Seeing and believing without doing the work will not produce success!

Begin sharing your dream with those who love and support you. This may be your parents, grandparents, a sibling, or another relative. Some of your biggest supporters may be those who aren't relatives, such as a teacher, pastor, neighbor, or one of your friends. Share those dreams so you can have your team of supporters who will hold you accountable to do the work. One thing you want to avoid is telling your dreams to those who really don't support you. I warn you that everyone will not encourage you to pursue your dreams and goals.

Some may want to see you accomplish your dreams, but they will hate on you because they don't want to dedicate to putting in the work to get it done. Don't let the weight of your haters keep you down, but let it lift you up. Let it fuel the fire in you! You may find that some people will try to discourage you and do whatever they can to prevent you from moving forward in accomplishing your dreams. Little sisters, please do not let this discourage you, and use it as a driving force. Sometimes the road to accomplishing your dream may seem a little lonely and scary, but just know that you and the Lord are more than enough!

Write down those dreams and pray to the Lord about your dreams. Pursue your dreams with passion. You can do and be anything that you dream of. It may take hard work and dedication with sacrifice, but you can do it. When nobody else believes in your dreams, it will be during this time that you double down and continue in pursuit, according to Philippians 4:13, "you can do all things through Christ who gives you strength."

You are very precious in the sight of the Lord, so dream on and work hard to get those dreams accomplished and watch and see how the Lord God will do it. They that wait upon the Lord, He shall renew your strength (Isaiah 40:31). I'm proud of the blessings that our Heavenly Father will do for you and through you when you bring your dreams before Him in prayer and keep the faith and work to accomplish them. He will provide you with everything that you will need. I'm here to cheer you on.

As a young girl who grew up in a single-parent home, in a neighborhood where drugs were used and sold, I'm a testimony that God blessed me to overcome the odds that were stacked against me. Some people believe that individuals are a product of their environment; therefore, if you grow up in poverty there is a very high possibility that you will reside in poverty. But then again, if God is on your side, the expectation of a good outcome exceeds the possibility of you succumbing to the circumstances of your environment. By the grace of our Lord God, He blessed me to make it out.

God blessed me to surpass getting a bachelor's degree. I went on to get a master's and then a doctorate degree. I'm thankful to Jesus for the prayers and support of so many who encouraged me to never give up on my dreams and continue believing and receiving so many blessings of the Lord. Just as God blessed me, He will do the same for you. Therefore, I encourage you to keep dreaming and believing in your goals. Talk to the Father, our Lord, about your dreams and how you will use them to be a blessing to others, and as you anticipate achieving your dreams you will see in amazement how He transforms life for you just as He did for me.

Blessed in the Skin I'm In

I LOVE THE SKIN I'M IN

My beloved little sisters, the very essence of your beauty is from within. Being blessed in the skin that you're in doesn't necessarily involve your physical appearance or swag. You've probably heard the familiar saying, "Beauty is only skin deep." Therefore, in this context, being blessed in the skin that you're in simply means your focus is on knowing who you are in the Lord. You must be internally grateful for who you are in our eternal God.

You are uniquely made; therefore, rejoice in being your authentic self. No one can look, feel, or act exactly as you. Our Creator has made you for His good pleasure and has blessed you to be a blessing just as you are. Being blessed in the skin that you're in is not based on your color, race, or creed. It's not influenced by your height, weight, or body shape. You're blessed in the skin that you are in to establish healthy relationships with others. You must first allow yourself to learn who you are, love and receive love from those who support you and have your best interest at heart. Guard your heart as you establish boundaries for those who interact with you, and always take the high road and walk away from toxic people or situations.

You, individually and absolutely, are precious in the sight of God! Being blessed in the skin that you're in focuses on your character, integrity, and energy, which are all valuable and precious in God's sight. Everything that the Lord has made, it is good. That includes you. So embrace you, and walk in the blessed skin that you're in. Welcome the Father's spirit and embrace His anointing as it flows through and within you and everything that you do.

The God of all creation fashioned and formed you when you were in your mother's womb, and you were made to be a fabulous creation! According to Jeremiah 1:5, "Before I formed you in the womb I knew you, and before you were born I consecrated you; I appointed you a prophet to the nations." Young sister, before you were born, our God set you apart and called you by His grace (Galatians 1:15 ESV). The Lord looks and examines your heart, not how pretty you are. Too many girls and young ladies put more emphasis on being pretty and cute, as their most important focus. But the Lord wants us to understand that our true beauty comes from within. The First Epistle of Peter 3:3–4 says, "Your beauty should not come from outward adornment, such as elaborate hairstyles and the wearing of gold jewelry or fine clothes. Rather, it should be that of your inner self, the unfading beauty of a gentle and quiet spirit, which is of great worth in God's sight."

Your body is a temple made by God and for God. Therefore, everything that you do with and to your body is important. The Bible says in 1 Corinthians 6:19, "Do you not know that your bodies are temples of the Holy Spirit, who is in you, whom you have received from God? You are not your own." This means that you must be careful not to engage in things that are sinful with your bodies, such as having sexual relations before marriage, hurting yourself, and putting yourself in dangerous situations that may cause you harm.

Designed for Generational Blessings

According to Genesis 12:1–3 (NIV), "The Lord had said to Abram, 'Go from your country, your people and your father's household to the land I will show you. I will make you into a great nation, and I will bless you; I will make your name great, and you will be a blessing. I will bless those who bless you, and whoever curses you I will curse; and all peoples on earth will be blessed through you.'" Our God has no respect for persons, and you too are a blessing, young sister. You are a blessing to your family. Perhaps at times you may not feel like you are a blessing to your family, and unfortunately, there may be times wherein they might not treat you as such, nevertheless, you are a blessing!

You must hold on to every word of God for your life. According to Psalm 127:3, "Children are a gift from the

Lord. They are a reward from him." Simply stated, you are a gift from God to your family. As a gift and blessing to your family, if there is conflict, chaos, or challenges happening in your family, you can let them see the Spirit of God working in you and through you to help restore unity. As a believer in the Lord, you can share with your family what God is doing in your life. You can be a witness in your family to let them know that the blessings of God are upon you, and He has the best plan for your life. Your family will see that it doesn't matter what happened generations before you, great things are being birthed in you because the hand of the Lord is upon you as you are a new creature and are renewed in our Lord and Savior Jesus Christ. God has a remnant in you.

Generational blessings are moving forth in you and through you. You can share with those around you that our Great God is giving you peace and rest even in challenging times. You have on the inside of you what it takes to be the difference in your family, especially those who may not be believers. You can ask the Lord to send down His blessings on your family so that things change for many generations to come, especially if you have younger siblings. God doesn't want you to hide the blessings and favor that He's pouring into you from your family, especially younger children. Share with the generations to come, all the praises of the Lord and His strength and His wonderful works that He has done (Psalm 78:4).

Has there been any time when you wished that you were connected to some other family? If so, you are not the first person to feel this way, and you won't be the last. Sometimes people gaze at other families and ponder their

Flowing in Favor

successes and desire the same for their family. They may wish their family thrived as others based on what they see or hear, but realistically all families at some point experience challenges. That includes those families that appear to have it all together. Don't be deceived by the houses, cars, bling, and fame. Truth is, there is no perfect family.

If you are assessing the blessings of other families based on what you see on social media or gossip of others, don't believe the hype, nor evaluate your family based on what the Lord has done for others. Riches and fame don't give everlasting joy or peace, and it has nothing to do with eternal life in Jesus Christ. If there is conflict or strife in your family, let it end with you. You are the next generation of blessings in your family. May the peace of God abide in you forevermore. Remember, all families are different. In some families, there are two parents, and in others, there are single parents. You may have parents who've decided it is best to co-parent, but it doesn't mean that your family is any less blessed.

Your life should be a living example of the great and mighty things that the Lord is doing. Every morning that God blesses you to wake up is another incredible opportunity for you to make a difference in your family and our world. You're not too young to make a positive impact in your family members' lives. Let the Lord use you to be the one who restores life and healing for all those who come into your presence as you share the goodness of the Lord in your life.

Stay on the right track so you can avoid unnecessary collisions.

Love Your Peace

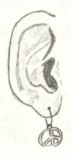

Love yourself and your peace! Your peace is so important, little sisters… Be an ambassador of your innermost peace and protect it at all costs. Satan, the enemy of God, is in constant pursuit of robbing you of peace. But the Lord did not leave us without the knowledge, power, and ability to defeat anything that tries to take our peace. So today is a perfect day for you to decide, determine, and declare that the peace of God rests upon you. Having peace doesn't mean that you won't have challenges or troubles. In fact, that's the beauty of the awesome peace that only the Lord gives. The Lord Jehovah gives us peace that can eradicate anything that comes against us. No matter what you experience, our God can give you peace to overcome it.

From this point on, tell yourself, "I am wonderfully and fearfully made in the Lord; and our souls know this right well," according to Psalm 139. Do you love yourself? If so, when was the last time that you told yourself that you love yourself? It's awesome for you to love yourself. I'm encouraging you and thanking you for loving who you are. You are a child of God, and the Lord God doesn't make any mistakes.

God formed and fashioned you in your mother's womb before you came into this world. He created you to be all that you should be in Him, and you are a blessing. God loves you so much that He gave His only Son, Jesus Christ, as a sacrifice for you. We were all born in sin, and when we were born, we were already sinners, but Jesus's precious life and blood was given to cover our sins and free us, and that is all we need. So praise Jesus for what He has done. Through the blood of Jesus, as you trust and believe in Him, you will be saved from your sins, praise God! I'm so glad to be born again and have a Savior who died for me. What about you?

If you love yourself, little sister, please take care of yourself. This means that you take time for yourself so you can have peace and joy, and it may be well with your soul. If you feel overwhelmed with too many responsibilities from school, activities, or other commitments, do not be afraid to let your parents know. Even when pressured by friends to hang out and you must decline because of other obligations, do not allow it to cause you emotional fatigue. Just say no, and let your no mean *no*. You are responsible for your peace, so take comfort in not letting others disturb it. Declutter your mind, and keep it free from any negative thinking, feelings, ideas, or anything that may keep you from growing in the grace and knowledge of our Lord. Our minds are one of the first areas that Satan tries to influence us. Ask the Lord daily to clothe you in peace and humility; and He will do just that.

Growing in Grace

Growing in grace is such a beautiful process! Throughout your adolescence and young adulthood, you will be continuously discovering who you are. You are uncovering the beauty of the Lord in your life and taking responsibility for Him to lead the way for you. I'm confident that as you are growing in grace and seeking the Lord and all His righteousness for your life, He will direct your path. As you grow in grace, you no longer look just for what God can do for you, but you begin to focus on what you can do for the Lord. It is the Lord who abides in you and grows you in His grace and knowledge if your heart desires to do so. Just as the things around us grow and mature, God has poised you with the ability to flourish through Him in the fruits of the spirit, through love, joy,

Flowing in Favor

hope, peace, faith, goodness, meekness, and self-control, against such there is no law (Galatians 5:22–23).

Don't seek popularity, especially if it is a consequence of sin. Doing things that are hurtful or offensive to others so you can be popular is sinful, even if it's self-inflicted harm.

It's such a great feeling when we as individuals know that we are walking in the path of God. You are uniquely created by God, and as you grow in His grace, you will recognize the importance of being obedient to His will for your life. As you grow in God's grace, you will make a difference everywhere that you go.

As you grow in grace and avail yourself to be used by the Lord, He will put you in settings where your presence will change the atmosphere to one which is positive, encouraging, and prosperous. At home, school, practice, or in extracurricular activities, His grace will motivate you in being patient, considerate, and will prevent you from popping off when things do not go your way or as you think they should. You grow in grace by reading God's Word and meditating on scripture to be knowledgeable of His will for you in all circumstances. Think of it this way, when you grow in God's grace, you are sprouting in your relationship with our Lord and Savior. Therefore, give glory to God, because even though in age you are a young person, spiritually you are fully developing as a mature Christian in the body of Christ.

When you think about God's amazing grace, it is so incredible. Although we deserve punishment for our sins, He freely demonstrates mercy, goodness, and blessings to us. Ephesians 2:8–9 reads, "For by grace you have been saved through faith. And this is not your own doing; it is the gift of God." Likewise, we should also show characteristics of grace to others, such as forgiveness, patience, and love. Having patience with yourself and others is so important. Don't beat yourself up or take on unnecessary stress when you attempt to accomplish something, and it takes a little longer than you or others think it should. Let grace in God's perfect timing bloom and flow in your life according to His plan for you.

God's grace is not given to you because you have been so honest, obedient, or loving. Despite our faults and failures, He looks beyond our flaws and abundantly meets our needs. The Holy Spirit may nudge you to do what is right even when others are trying to entice you to do something wrong. Take heed and give thanks for a gracious God who provides for our needs even when we may not ask.

Healing for a Heavy Heart

Having a heavy heart can happen to anyone at any time for many reasons. When speaking of having a heavy heart, this refers to someone feeling really saddened about a person, place, thing, or situation. It's very important to deal with a heavy or broken heart because it may disturb your spirit and can lead to depression or perhaps other emotional, physical, or mental issues. Signs and symptoms of a heavy heart can include feeling down, feeling alone, feeling hopeless, crying, feeling worthless, and feeling empty. You may not feel like eating. You may find yourself not making the best decisions based on whatever is causing the heaviness of heart and troubling of your spirit.

Clinically speaking, if someone doesn't deal with or handle a heavy heart they may find themselves getting depressed. According to Cambridge University Press (n.d.

2023), clinical depression refers to someone who has a form of mental illness that is associated with emotions of sadness and hopelessness which may interrupt their normal activities of daily living, such as eating, sleeping, toileting, and socializing. Perhaps you have never experienced heaviness of heart but have known someone who has. Jesus can give you rest for your heavy heart. Cast all your care upon Him, because He cares for you (1 Peter 5:7).

Satan is the author of confusion, and he doesn't want you to see that there is a resolution for handling every problem. There is no problem, burden, or situation that our God cannot handle. It is important for you to know that your parents or guardians can help you deal with your heavy heart. Jesus says He will give you rest if you put your trust in Him (Matthew 11:28). A lot of times, we think we are alone and no one knows what we are going through, but the Bible tells us that God is omniscient, which means He is aware of your situation, because He knows everything. Whenever our hearts in self-accusation make us feel guilty and condemn us, know that we are always in God's hands. God is above and greater than our consciences, and He knows everything. Nothing is hidden from Him.

Do not allow resentment to form in your heart against those who should have protected you from the pain that you may have experienced. Perhaps they didn't know what to do in protecting you. Some dysfunctional situations are the result of generational curses that have been passed down. Adults sometimes have difficulty making the right decisions because of their painful past or emotional trauma they're struggling with, and therefore they may have been unsure about or unable to appropriately help you. Although it's difficult for you as a young person to understand, because you feel adults should have it altogether, that's not exactly true for everyone. Some adults have suffered abuses which has left them fractured or broken, and they have yet to experience healing. They can't help you if they can't help themselves. So release them and the resentment, so your emotions can heal and this cycle can be broken.

Listen for the still, small voice which is the prompting of the Holy Spirit to guide you when you experience a heavy or broken heart. When you are feeling deeply saddened, please believe that the Lord is right there with you. Call on the name of Jesus and pour your heart out to Him. Satan wants you to feel alone and that no one cares, but the devil is a liar! You are never alone! We serve a God who is omnipresent, in other words, He is everywhere at the same time. In fact, this is a perfect time for you to open your Bible and check out Psalm 139. Rehearse these beautiful verses and keep them tucked in your heart, because the Lord knows your heart and He loves you. Also, I want to encourage you that sometimes your setbacks are setups for you to be blessed.

Your life is meaningful, and your worth is precious to the Lord. He has a purpose and plan for your life. No matter what you go through, as long as you have breath in your body, your life is worth living. The Lord will guide you to accomplish the plans and purpose He has in you. The Father has not forgotten about you, no matter what anyone thinks. Proverbs 15:3 states, "The eyes of the Lord are in every place, keeping watch on the evil and the good."

Forgiveness for Me

Forgiveness is for you. It is so important that you know you have been made for the greater good. Satan wants you to hold on to bitterness, hate, anger, envy, hurt, and pain. This is because the enemy knows that once you let go of these negative emotions, you will be free. Forgiveness is not for the person that hurt you; it's for you to be free. For you to survive and live in complete healing and total freedom, you must forgive. It may be uncomfortable to think about the one who took advantage of you, but God will give you the strength as an overcomer, in the mighty name of Jesus!

Forgiveness means *you* must forgive *you*! Perhaps you're holding on to things that are or were beyond your control, and you feel guilt or shame because the outcomes were a result of your ignorance. Perhaps you were disobedient and feel this contributed to things you've experienced. Pray,

Flowing in Favor

give it to the Lord our God, and forgive yourself. Wrap your arms around your shoulders, thank the Lord for loving you, and tell yourself that you love you. Look in the mirror and speak to yourself, girl. You are loved and you will be okay.

Sometimes, the pressure from hurtful people and experiences have kept you emotionally captive. As you try to cope with the pain, guilt, and shame, at times it may become overwhelming because the enemy will try to slowly rob you of your peace. Remember, you win because you chose to forgive and be loosed from bondage. That person cannot harm or hurt you anymore once you forgive them. It is in God's will for you to be delivered from every offense, so forgive and be free in Jesus's name!

You have repressed that situation for too long, little sister. Don't develop resentment in your heart for those who should have protected you, but didn't, for whatever reason. Perhaps they may not have known how to protect you, or tried and didn't do as well as you deserved. Unfortunately, some dysfunctional behaviors from grown folks are the result of circumstances or generational issues that have been passed down, and they don't understand that their behavior is dysfunctional, toxic, and causes more hurt and pain for those they are supposed to care for and protect from harm. If this is your story, understand that you can be the change agent in your small circle of influence by avoiding making bad decisions that hurt others.

You will be a positive influence for your generation to encourage them to not allow people or situations to manipulate them into believing those things have dominion over their destiny. God made you special to be successful in completing His kingdom work. Yes, you may have cried, but God is wiping those tears. Take flight from every situation that has tried to limit the anointing that is upon you; just as birds fly to higher heights, so will you with your head held high, looking toward the heavens, thanking the Lord our God who gives you favor to triumph in forgiveness in Jesus's Name. Praise God for your supernatural ability to forgive despite how you may feel. You are right; you cannot do it by yourself, but you can do it with the guidance and support of the Lord our Mighty God.

Dear sweet daughter, when the disciple Peter went to Jesus about forgiveness, he asked Jesus should he forgive his brother who sinned against him seven times? Jesus told him that he should forgive not just seven times, but seventy times seven (Matthew 18:21–22). This same rule applies to us too. Your breakthrough is in your forgiveness. It doesn't matter if you're in juvenile detention; you will not be imprisoned in your mind, because the Lord will help you to forgive and walk in love, joy, peace, and patience.

The Lord doesn't want you to worry or spazz about anything. You may be thinking, "Yeah right, she doesn't know my situation." You're correct, but I do know the One who knows everything about you from your past to your present. The Bible says that the Lord knows every hair strand that is upon our head, and our worth is valuable to Him (Matthew 10:30). Don't let the pain or hurt that you have experienced take root in you and cause you to bring harm or suffering to others. Pray the Father removes the bullying, hate, fighting, and scars from your heart and mind. Choose this day to forgive for you!

Flowing in Favor

By means of forgiveness, we pray for others who have spoken or gossiped about us untruthfully. Little sister, consider this adage, "Hurt people have a habit of wounding other people." This is because they are likely caught up in a web of hurt, guilt, or shame. If you've been blessed to survive the insensitive, hurtful, and inappropriate behavior that someone else has inflicted upon you, ask the Father to give you the strength to forgive and be released from the anguish and pain that you may have endured. We don't benefit from being spiteful or retaliating as if we will have a one-up. This behavior only gives temporary relief, and the devil gets an advantage, not God.

Forgiveness is a benefit to you; therefore, do not take revenge, my dear little sisters. Pray for God's mercy on others who may have hurt you because He will fight your battles as it is written, "Vengeance is mine. I will repay," says the Lord. Hatred and bitterness are not solutions, and they unquestionably lead to bigger problems. Remember this, when you release forgiveness, you win, *period*!

Respect Yourself and Others

Respect yourself and others. You must hold yourself accountable to do and say what is right because this is the will of God for all our lives. If you want others to respect you, then you first must respect yourself. Be mindful of what you say and how you say it. You may say the right thing, but incorrectly. It's important that you understand "it's not what you say, it's how you say it." For instance, when you try to get your point across to anyone, you do not need to use profanity, shout, or overtalk the person. Using profanity isn't cute, and you get more respect without using profane words anyway.

Likewise, be mindful of your behavior. Think before you act. Stop popping off every time someone says or does something that rubs you the wrong way. You don't want to be labeled as one who stays on edge. In other words, you don't want to behave as if you're a bomb ready to explode at any given second from the simplest thing that may tick you off. According to Psalm 119:9, "How can a young person stay on the path of purity? By living according to God's word." Sometimes you may find yourself in a situation where you feel a person doesn't deserve respect. Particularly, you should think about the situation from a godly perspective. Give respect and insist that others respect you too.

Young queens, it is my prayer that you realize how much of a blessing you are to the Father. God put something special inside of you. And no one else has it, nor can they duplicate it. Don't let your ego or emotions control you and cause you to lose focus. Let your reactions be respectful. The Lord will preserve and keep you from sins of the flesh and things that are ungodly. For that reason, be thoughtful of the words that you say, and do not be distracted by being popular. That is, do not put your reputation at risk doing ungodly things that might bring about negative consequences.

Respect the rules and authority in your home, school, church, and other places as it may be required. If your friends try to persuade you to do things that are evil, dishonest, or contrary to what is right in God's sight, do not follow them. Don't let those who prefer to walk in darkness lead you as if you are blind and don't have a clue. You are a child of the Light for the Kingdom of God.

Choose to do what is right. Think about the consequences before you do wrong, because our God is all-seeing and all-knowing. Before jumping and doing things that are morally and socially inappropriate, such as lying, stealing, cheating, fighting, having sexual relations, being disobedient, or destroying property, take a few moments to think about the consequences with both man and God. Some repercussions last a long time, perhaps years and possibly one's lifetime. It's easy to get into trouble; it may be very hard to get out of it. There is no respect in getting into trouble.

Put your name here, "I _____ will respect myself and others!"

Friendships

Being a good steward and demonstrating camaraderie is important. This means that you look to inspire others around you, especially when they are doing the right thing. Don't be a hater. Cheer others on who are doing well, and let it be well with your soul. It's good when you can empower others to reach and accomplish their goals, especially when they do what's right for Christ. In 1 Thessalonians 5:11 (NLT), we read, "So encourage each other and build each other up, just as you are already doing." You are blessed to be a blessing! If you feel that others are progressing and you haven't reached your goals don't get disappointed. You keep your eye on the prize and strive to thrive.

Run your race and help someone along the way. It's important to always lend a helping hand when you can. Today, make the decision to be the positive energy in your friendship circle. This will be fulfilling for you, and the energy will spread to your friends like butter on sliced bread. My mother always said, "What goes around comes around." In other words, what you do for others will be done for you. Encourage your friends and associates, and if you have an opportunity to share pearls of wisdom with them to enlighten them, challenge yourself to do it. Team up with your peers to make the road ahead easier for yourself and others.

When your friends or others flake out on you, continue to focus on what you need to succeed. If you feel ignored by others, remind yourself that God will never leave you. Early in life, you must understand that relationships come and go, so choose friends wisely. Some people are in your life for only a season, so imagine the best for the situation and avoid drama or unnecessary worries with things you cannot change. Just imagine that you are never alone, and God is a friend that will be with you no matter what.

Many are going to cross your path on your journey. Some will walk with you, and others will walk away from you. In school, you may develop bonds with others and find that some will have your back while others ghost you. A friend will support you to the end while you are on your journey. Your BFFs are those who will celebrate with you during your successes and comfort you during your failures. Be grateful for godly friendships that are meaningful in which you and your friends are on one accord in the Lord.

Have you ever heard the phrase "Birds of a feather flock together"? That's something my mom would always tell me. She would repeatedly say, "Whoever you are hanging out with will either have an influence on you, or you will have an influence on them." If your friends are unpleasant, rebellious, or rambunctious, they will expect you to be the same. And if you decide to hang out and go along for the ride just to become a part of the clique, unfortunately, you're guilty by association.

It's important for you to stay away from friendships with those who are rebellious and disobedient to their parents or disrespectful to others. Closely observe and flee from any bestie who chooses to have a bad attitude or prefers negative energy. You should not feel guilty about taking a break or distancing yourself from friends who are doing the most by acting out. Your friends should be courteous, not bullies. And your best friends should promote hope, not hate.

A Prayer for Godly Friendships

Dear heavenly Father, my prayer is that You would forgive me of my sins and all unrighteousness. Thank You for Your grace and mercy. Please lead and guide me to choose the right friends, those who love You. The Bible says, "Sweet friendships refresh the soul and awaken our hearts with joy, for good friends are like the anointing oil that yields the fragrant incense of God's presence," (Proverbs 27:9 TPT). Help me to love and always be a blessing to my friends. Help me to encourage and support them to do what is right. I thank You for blessing me with friends that I currently have and those to come in Jesus's name. Amen!

Acts of Kindness

There is no harm in being kind. My mother often reminded me, "What goes around comes around." Acts of kindness imply your actions are thoughtful of others. And He that holds your future is pleased when you show kindness to others. Colossians 3:12 states, "Put on then, as God's chosen ones, holy and beloved, compassionate hearts, kindness, humility, meekness, and patience." And guess what, I believe if you continue to show acts of kindness letting God's love rule in your heart, you will begin to have increased love in your heart also.

A soft answer turns away wrath, but a harsh word stirs up anger (Proverbs 15:1 NKJV). So be mindful of not only what you do, but also what you say. Some people may think being kind means you let others walk all over you or treat you like crap. That is undeniably far from the truth.

Flowing in Favor

Perhaps you've tried to be kind to others and they took advantage of you. If this is your truth, I urge you to search your heart and make a conscious decision to reflect on the past and let it be just that. It is your past; it is behind you, and you are presently living your best life on purpose for God.

Some folks think it's impossible to be kind, or we don't have to be kind, but this is not what Jesus said about being kind. In Luke 6:35 it states, "But love your enemies, and do good, and lend, expecting nothing in return, and your reward will be great, and you will be sons of the Most High, for He is kind to the ungrateful and the evil." The Father sets high standards for His children because He knows that through Jesus Christ we can *do all things* because He gives us the strength (Philippians 4:13). You will also read in the Word of God that "Love is patient, love is kind. It does not envy, it does not boast, it is not proud. It does not dishonor others, it is not self-seeking, it is not easily angered, it keeps no record of wrongs. Love does not delight in evil but rejoices with the truth. It always protects, always trusts, always hopes, always perseveres" (1 Corinthians 13:4–7). Yes, you are a holy creation and you're flowing in the favor of God! God is love! For this reason, you are created to show acts of kindness because you are a child of God.

Academic Success

Destined for greatness!

Your academic mission is not impossible! Academic success is yours if you pursue it. To pursue means that you will wholeheartedly chase after and engage in the necessary work to achieve academic success. Run your race and focus on being the best student that you can be. If you are in school, what are your grades? Hopefully, you're striving to reach the moon so that you can land on or surpass the stars. What do you want your average grade to be? Are you satisfied with *A*s, *B*s, or *C*s? What are you doing to ensure you get the grade that you so desire? Think about your study habits, and what drives you to succeed. How often do you grind to make a high grade on a test, quiz, or homework assignment? Be sure that you maintain good study habits.

For some students, studying and retaining information comes very easily, and they thrive in school and make very high grades. But for others, including myself when I attended school, there may be some challenges that must be overcome. I had to work hard by consistently reading, taking notes, and using other resources to remember and apply knowledge so I could attain academic success. Reflect on your study habits, and what efforts you've harnessed that may contribute to your academic success. Do you have a good relationship with your teachers or instructors? Do you need tutoring or use resources that may be available to you? If not, why?

Academic success may come with challenges or sacrifices, but you are made for it. Remember, you can do all things through Christ who gives you strength (Philippians 4:13). In the end, you will win if you pray, keep the faith, and be consistent in what you have set your mind to. You will see over time the major changes and improvement that you make through prayer, faith, and consistency will work in your favor. Why? Because you understand the importance of prayer, faith, and consistency in your academic achievement.

Be relentless in your efforts, and the God who sees and hears will allow you to successfully pass that class or semester. When you're in class, learn all that you can. Do not disrupt or disrespect your teacher. Yes, if you don't quit, you will finish what you have started. Continue praying, believing, and putting in the work. It will pay off; I'm a living testimony.

Principle: Always pray before studying, testing, quizzing, presenting, or anything that you must rely on information to come across successfully.

Destined for Greatness

(handwritten: Destined for Greatness!)

You are destined for greatness! And you are flowing in the favor of God. Each morning as you awake and embark on a new day that our all-knowing God has created, you must speak to the spirit within. Tell yourself, "Being confident of this very thing, that He who has begun a good work in me will complete it until the day of Jesus Christ" (Philippians 1:6). Before you were born, God knew you! In fact, the Bible lets us know that the Lord knew exactly who you would be before He formed you in the womb, and before you were born, He set you apart. The Lord appointed you as a prophet to the nations (Jeremiah 1:5 NIV). This simply means that the Lord our God is the orchestrator of your life, and He uniquely designed you for the designated work and plans that may impact society through using your kingdom gifts for His work. Therefore, the most important thing and best decision that you can make is to have a personal relationship with Jesus Christ.

Although you are a youth, you are precious in the sight of our Lord. Therefore, my blessed and favored young sister, enjoy your youth. Have fun and make sure you have a happy adolescence. Do not stress or be overwhelmed about adult things. Excite yourself with good pleasures that will enhance your formative years. You only get one shot at being a youth, so shoot your best shot! Yesterday is not recorded, which means you will never get a chance to repeat it. Tomorrow is not promised, therefore spring forth today and make the best out of every moment that our Great God gives you to experience His supernatural joy, peace, love, and favor.

Just think, if you created something, no other person would know more about your creation than you. Even if you gave them the plans of your creation, you get the accolades and advantage. More importantly, the Father and Creator of you is making, molding, and shaping you for greater. So be very sure to let the One and only true God be in your life to lead you and guide you throughout your life. When you realize how good God's mercy is and reflect on how great He is, it will fuel you to hold Him and never let go. And guess what, if you keep your mind stayed on Him, the Lord will keep you in perfect peace (Isaiah 26:3). Keep your heart open to the Lord, and He will abide in you and you in Him forevermore.

Embrace your youth with optimism with faith in the Lord our God who has your life in His hands. Don't accept anyone's negative comments or actions about your future. Instead, continue to be inspired on your journey of living, learning, and loving experiences that will influence your destination and encapsulate the flow of God's favor in your life.

I'm sure as you reflect on what you've read and pondered in your heart all the great things about your Heavenly Father and the blessings that are yet to come into your life and throughout your life, keep seeking godly wisdom and being obedient to the Father and flow in His favor in Jesus's name! May God grant you increased faith in His Word when you experience obstacles. May He grant you fervor and vision to pursue your passions and use your gifts and talents for His Kingdom purpose. And may the Father grant you favor multiplied with wisdom and provision that flows like a thunderous waterfall to complete every good work that is in your heart.

Scriptures to Ponder

ROMANS
ACTS
JOHN
LUKE
MARK
MATTHEW

In the beginning was the Word, and the Word was with God and the Word was God. He was with God in the beginning. Through him all things were made; without him nothing was made that has been made. In him was life, and that life was the light of men. The light shines in the darkness, but the darkness has not understood it. (John 1:1–5)

For God so loved the world that he gave his one and only Son, that whoever believes in him shall not perish but have eternal life. For God did not send his Son into the world to condemn the world, but to save the world through him. (John 3:16–17)

But seek first his kingdom and his righteousness, and all these things will be given to you as well. (Matthew 6:33)

That if you confess with your mouth, "Jesus is Lord," and believe in your heart that God raised him from the dead, you will be saved. For it is with your heart that you believe and are justified, and it is with your mouth that you confess and are saved. (Roman 10:9–10)

Children, obey your parents in the Lord, for this is right. "Honor your father and mother"—which is the first commandment with a promise, "that it may go well with you and that you may enjoy long life on the earth." (Ephesians 6:1–3)

Trust in the Lord with all your heart and lean not on your own understanding, in all your ways acknowledge him, and he will make your paths straight. (Proverbs 3:5–6)

I can do all things through Christ who gives me strength. (Philippians 4:13 KJV)

Flowing in Favor

Don't let anyone look down on you because you are young, but set an example for the believers in speech, in conduct, in love, in faith and in purity. (1 Timothy 4:12 NIV)

"For I know the plans I have for you," declares the Lord, "Plans to prosper you and not to harm you, plans to give you a hope and a future." (Jeremiah 29:11)

I praise you because I am fearfully and wonderfully made; your works are wonderful, I know that full well. (Psalm 139:14)

I will bless the Lord at all times: his praise hall continually be in my mouth. (Psalm 34:1–2)

Come, ye children, hearken unto me: I will teach you the fear of the Lord. (Psalm 34:11)

Your beauty should not come from outward adornment, such as braided hair and the wearing of gold jewelry and fine clothes. 4 Instead, it should be that of your inner self, the unfading beauty of a gentle and quiet spirit, which is of great worth in God's sight. (1 Peter 3:3–4)

Whoever dwells in the shelter of the Most High will rest in the shadow of the Almighty.

I will say of the Lord, "He is my refuge and my fortress, my God, in whom I trust." (Psalm 91:1–2 NIV)

Your word is a lamp unto my feet, and a light to my path. (Psalm 119:105 KJV)

Now unto him that is able to do exceeding abundantly above all that we ask or think, according to the power that worketh in us. 21 Unto him be glory in the church by Christ Jesus throughout all ages, world without end. Amen. (Ephesians 3:20 KJV)

It is recommended that you carefully reflect on what you've read and begin journaling in this section how you will improve yourself today for a better tomorrow.

Conclusion

Dearly beloved little sisters, you are worth the investment! My desire is that this book inspires you to be all that the Lord has made you to be. Embrace your journey with faith in the true and living God. Let your life be a light that guides others from darkness as peace, love, joy, and forgiveness shine brightly through you into the world. And may your faith, commitment, and love for Jesus propel you to higher heights in your spiritual growth, grace, and greatness!

References

Cambridge University Press. (ND.) "Upcycling." In *Cambridge Dictionary*. Retrieved December 21, 2023 from https://dictionary.cambridge.org/us/dictionary/english/upcycling.

Holy Bible, Keystone Giant Print Presentation Edition: King James Version. National Bibles. National Publishing. January 1, 1997.

New International Version. Bible Gateway, https://www.biblegateway.com/versions/New-International-Version-NIV-Bible/#booklist. Accessed 20 October 2023.

Contact info:
Karen Powell
Krobins66@yahoo.com
281-744-8224

About the Author

Karen Powell is the wife of Mr. Cloyd Powell, who has lovingly inspired and supported her to pursue her passions. She is the mother of Teren Marie and six other wonderful children by marriage: Xavier, Joy, Demond, Tiffany, Jessica, and Yvette. She loves the Lord, and her soul says, "I will bless the Lord at all times and His praises shall continually be within my mouth," which is her favorite scripture (Psalm 34:1).

As a young woman, Karen started this journey saying yes to the Lord to work in ministry. She became an intercessor of prayer at the age of twenty-five years old and has remained faithful to the 5 a.m. Prayer Line for thirty-two years. She was involved at her former church, True Vine Missionary BC in New Orleans, as a Youth Bible School teacher and faithfully served in the Women of Faith Ministry before relocating to Texas. She loves to inspire youth to trust God and be all that they can be. She's been a speaker at numerous women's ministries. She's a committed servant to Apouringin2 Ministry for Children and Families, and A Woman of Godly Influence (AWOGI) ministry, where she uses her gifts and talents in ministry. She has rightfully earned her doctorate degree in nursing, where she is an adjunct professor and serves in a leadership role at a hospital in the Texas Medical Center. Wholeheartedly, she feels she's blessed to be a blessing!

Printed in the USA
CPSIA information can be obtained
at www.ICGtesting.com
CBHW021747050924
13881CB00041B/590